ENGLISH

Back to Basics

Classroom and Homework Activities

word study

punctuation

spelling

grammar

Jenni Harrold

6311UK

Published by R.I.C. Publications® 2010

Republished under licence by Prim-Ed Publishing® 2010

Copyright© Jenni Harrold 2010

ISBN 978-1-84654-243-5

PR– 6311UK

Titles available in this series:

English – Back To Basics (Yr 1/P 2)
English – Back To Basics (Yr 2/P 3)
English – Back To Basics (Yr 3/P 4)
English – Back To Basics (Yr 4/P 5)
English – Back To Basics (Yr 5/P 6)
English – Back To Basics (Yr 6/P 7)
English – Back To Basics (Yr 6 Ext/S 1)

Internet websites

In some cases, websites or specific URLs may be recommended. While these are checked and rechecked at the time of publication, the publisher has no control over any subsequent changes which may be made to webpages. It is *strongly* recommended that the class teacher checks *all* URLs before allowing pupils to access them.

View all pages online

Website: www.prim-ed.com

English – Back To Basics is a comprehensive resource designed to teach and revise basic literacy concepts. Essential skills are covered in spelling and word study, punctuation and grammar; with phonics included in Books Yr 1/P 2, Yr 2/P 3 and Yr 3/P4. Each of the pages focuses on one concept, which is developed through relevant, graded activities.

Although intended as a homework series, these books are also ideal for:

- teaching a new concept
- consolidation
- assessment
- revision.

Titles in the series are:
English – Back To Basics – Yr 1/P 2
English – Back To Basics – Yr 2/P 3
English – Back To Basics – Yr 3/P 4
English – Back To Basics – Yr 4/P 5
English – Back To Basics – Yr 5/P 6
English – Back To Basics – Yr 6/P 7
English – Back To Basics – Yr 6 Ext/S 1

Contents

Teacher notes

Overview	iv
Curriculum links	v
Spelling and vocabulary lists	vi
Spelling rules	vi
Glossary	vii – xi
Additional word lists	xi
Vowel sounds	xii
Consonant sounds	xiii
Prefixes	xiv
Suffixes	xv
Word origins	xvi
Words commonly misspelt	xvii – xix
Words easily confused or misused	xx – xxi

Phonics

Initial sounds – 1	2–3
Initial sounds – 2	4–5
Final sounds – 1	6–7
Final sounds – 2	8–9
Middle sounds – 1	10–11
Middle sounds – 2	12–13
Initial links – bl, cl	14–15
Initial links – fl, gl	16–17
Initial links – pl, sl	18–19
Initial links – sw, tw	20–21
Initial links – cr, dr	22–23
Initial links – tr, sk	24–25
Initial links – sp, st	26–27
Final links – nt, ft	28–29
Final links – st, lt, pt	30–31
Final links – nd, ld	32–33
Final links – mp, lk	34–35
Final links – nk, sk	36–37
Final links – ff, ll, ss	38–39
Digraphs – ch	40–41
Digraphs – sh	42–43
Digraphs – th	44–45

Spelling and word study

Look, say, cover, write, check	46–47
Finding words	48–49
Words in words	50–51
Alphabetical order	52–53
Rhyming words	54–55
Opposites	56–57
Homophones	58–59

Punctuation

Capital letters – sentences	60–61
Capital letters – names	62–63
Full stops	64–65
Question marks	66–67
Editing	68–69

Grammar

Nouns	70–71
Verbs	72–73
Adjectives	74–75
Writing sentences – word order	76–77
Finishing sentences	78–79
Joining sentences – conjunctions	80–81
Writing sentences	82–83

Format

This series of books contains pupil and teacher pages focusing on skills in the following areas:

- spelling and word study
- punctuation
- grammar
- phonics (Books Yr 1/P 2, Yr 2/P 3 and Yr 3/P4).

Features

This series of books:

- provides activities on each page that relate to one literacy concept
- follows an organised format in which concepts are repeated and expanded across year levels
- uses a focal list of vocabulary
- has a pupil page supported by a corresponding teachers page
- has a teachers page that includes answers and detailed information explaining each concept
- provides additional reference information for teachers.

Purpose

This series of books is ideal for:

- teaching a new concept
- consolidating and revising knowledge and skills
- homework activities to revise skills taught in class
- assessment.

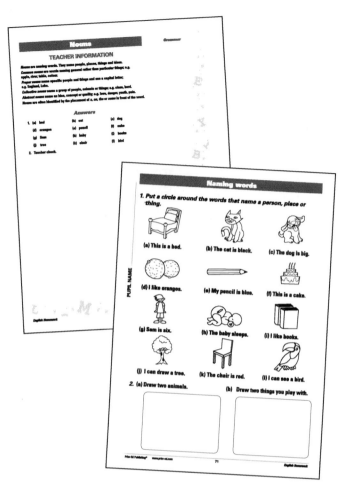

Spelling and vocabulary

There are two different lists of words used in each book:

- an age-appropriate spelling list of 40 words, and
- a high-frequency vocabulary list.

Both lists are used frequently throughout each book in the areas of spelling and word study, punctuation and grammar.

Additional reference material

This book includes:

- an extensive glossary of terms used in spelling and word study, punctuation and grammar
- vowel sounds and the different ways they are represented
- consonant sounds and the different ways they are represented
- spelling rules
- prefixes, their meanings and examples
- suffixes, their meanings and examples
- word origins – Latin and Greek root words with their meanings and examples
- words commonly misspelt
- words easily confused or misused
- prepositions and prepositional phrases
- words that can be used as adjectives or adverbs.

Country/Subject/Level	Curriculum Objectives
England Literacy Year One	**Word Recognition** • recognise an increasing number of familiar high frequency words • apply phonic knowledge and skills to reading and spelling **Word Structure and Spelling** • spell new words using phonics **Sentence Structure and Punctuation** • use capital letters and full stops
Northern Ireland Language and Literacy Foundation Stage and Key Stage One	**Foundation Stage – Talking and Listening** • develop phonological awareness and an extended vocabulary **Foundation Stage – Reading** • use word structure to develop reading • develop auditory and visual discrimination and memory **Key Stage One – Talking and Listening** • recognise features of language, showing phonological awareness **Key Stage One - Reading** • build up a sight vocabulary • identify words, patterns or letters • recognise and notice how words are constructed and spelt **Key Stage One - Writing** • use a variety of skills to spell words • spell correctly a range of familiar, important and regularly occurring words • develop increasing competence in the use of grammar and punctuation
Republic of Ireland English Senior Infants and First Class	**Senior Infants - Competence and Confidence in Using Language** • build up a sight vocabulary • learn to isolate the beginning and final sounds in written words • learn to isolate the part of a word or syllable which allows it to rhyme with another word or syllable • begin to develop conventional spelling **First Class – Receptiveness to Language** • continue to build a sight vocabulary • engage in activities designed to increase awareness of sounds • learn about the sounds associated with the part of a word or syllable that allows it to rhyme with another word or syllable • learn about the sounds associated with the beginning of a word or syllable • learn to connect the beginnings of words and syllables with their rhyming parts • learn about common word endings **First Class - Competence and Confidence in Using Language** • understand that the conventions of punctuation help to make meaning clearer in writing • spell words in a recognisable way based on an awareness of the most common spelling strings and patterns **First Class – Developing Cognitive Abilities through Language** • perform alphabetical order tasks
Scotland Literacy and English Early and First	**Early – Reading** • explore and play with the patterns and sounds of language and use what they learn • explore sounds, letters and words, discover how they work together and use them to help with reading and writing **Early – Writing** • explore sounds, letters and words, discover how they work together and use them to help with reading and writing **First – Reading** • use knowledge of sight vocabulary, phonics, punctuation and grammar to read with understanding and expression **First – Writing** • spell the most commonly-used words, using knowledge of letter patterns • write independently, use appropriate punctuation and order and link sentences in a way that makes sense
Wales Language, Literacy and Communication Skills Foundation Phase	**Reading - Skills** • understand that written symbols have sound and meaning and develop phonological, graphic and grammatical knowledge and word recognition **Writing - Skills** • recognise that punctuation is essential to help a reader understand what is written • develop ability to spell common and familiar words in a recognisable way

Spelling list

and	cat	go	it	on	was
am	dad	had	look	see	we
at	day	has	me	sit	wet
bed	did	I	mum	the	yes
big	dog	if	my	to	you
can	end	in	no	top	
car	get	is	of	up	

Vocabulary list

a	big	day	four	in	name	play	six	up
all	black	did	get	is	nine	purple	ten	was
am	blue	do	go	it	no	red	the	we
and	brown	dog	going	like	of	said	they	went
are	can	draw	green	look	on	see	this	white
at	cat	eight	grey	me	one	seven	three	yellow
away	come	five	he	mum	orange	she	to	yes
best	dad	for	I	my	pink	sit	two	you

Spelling rules

Write *i* before *e*, except after *c*.

> For example: friend, believe, receive, receipt

Some exceptions: foreign, either, science, weird, height, species

Write *ie* after *c* for words with a *shuhn* sound.

> For example: sufficient, ancient, conscience, efficient

Write *ei* when the vowel sounds like an *a*.

> For example: weigh, rein, reign, neighbour

For words ending in *y*:

- retain the *y* when adding *–ing*;
  for example: crying, studying
- retain the *y* if it is preceded by a vowel, when adding *s* or a suffix;
  for example: employs, employer
- change the *y* to *i* if it is preceded by a consonant, when adding a suffix;
  for example: cries, studies

Some exceptions: dryness, shyness.

Drop the final *e* to most words when adding a suffix beginning with a vowel.

> For example: use—usable
>   make—making

Double the consonant when adding a suffix starting with a vowel (e.g. -*ing*) to:

- a word of one syllable ending in a single consonant, preceded by a vowel;
  for example: drip—dripping
                sit—sitting
- a word of more than one syllable ending in a single consonant, preceded by a vowel *if* the stress is on the final syllable;
  for example: begin—beginning
                commit—committed.

When the stress is not on the final syllable, the single consonant remains;
for example: develop—developing—developed.

Exceptions include many words ending in *l*, where the *l* is always doubled;
for example: appal—appalling
              travel—travelling.

Abbreviation

An abbreviation is a word written in shortened form. A full stop may be used to show part of the word is missing. However, if the last letter of the word is used, there is no full stop.

For example: *Mon.* for Monday
Dr for Doctor

Acronym

A word made up from the initial letters of a phrase.

For example: *SIDS* (sudden infant death syndrome)
radar (radio detecting and ranging)

(Note: If it is not pronounced as a word, it is an intialism; e.g. *LPG*.)

Antonyms

Words that are opposite in meaning.

For example: *hot/cold*
dark/light
wet/dry

Base word

The root word or main part of the word. Prefixes and suffixes can be added to the base word.

For example: *read*ing, mis*guid*ed, *care*fully

Compound word

Two or more words joined together.

For example: *pancake, teaspoon, underground*

Consonant

Any letter of the alphabet that is not a vowel.

For example: *b, c, d, f, g, h, j*

Contraction

A shortened form of a word. An apostrophe is used to replace the deleted letters.

For example: *I'm, we're, they'll, she'd, can't*

Derivative

A word made from adding prefixes and suffixes to a base word.

For example: *sleep*ing, un*usual*, *happ*ily

Digraph

Two letters representing one phoneme.

For example: *th, sh, wh, er, ck, ou*

Eponyms

Eponyms are words that come from a person's name or name of a place.

For example: Jules *Leotard*
Anders *Celsius*
Earl of *Cardigan*

Etymology

The study of the origin and history of words.

For example: *annual* from the Latin word *annu*, meaning 'year'

Grapheme

The written representation of a sound.

For example: *ew, ing, th*

Homographs

Words that are spelt the same but have different origins and meanings and are sometimes pronounced differently.

For example: *cricket, wind*

Homophones

Words that sound the same but are spelled differently.

For example: *peace/piece*
threw/through
bored/board

Morpheme

The smallest unit of meaning.

For example: *house/keep/ing*

Phoneme

The smallest unit of sound in a word that can be represented by one, two, three or four letters. There are 44 phonemes in English.

For example: t*o*, sh*oe*, thr*ough*

Phonetics

System of spelling words that represents sounds by symbols.

Plural

Indicates more than one person or thing.

For example: two *books*
three *wishes*
four *children*

Prefix

Used at the beginning of a base word to change meaning.

For example: *in*edible, *un*conscious, *il*legal, *dis*obey

Singular

Only one person or thing.

For example: one *book,* a *table,* an *apple*

Suffix

Used at the end of a base word.

For example: work*ing,* lone*ly,* walk*ed,* edit*or*

Syllable

A unit of sound which contains a vowel sound. All words are made up of one or more syllables.

For example: talk, nerv-ous, in-de-pen-dent

Synonyms

Words that are similar in meaning.

For example: *big/large*
small/tiny
wet/damp

Thesaurus

A reference book which groups words by meaning.

For example: *promise*—pledge, guarantee, engagement, commit, assure, secure

Trigraph

Three letters representing one phoneme.

For example: h*igh*, fu*dge*, p*ear*

Vowel

The five letters of the alphabet that are not consonants.

These are: *a, e, i, o* and *u.*

Punctuation

Apostrophe

Used to show ownership and in contractions to show where letters have been dropped.

For example: Jackie's dog wasn't
                barking.

Capital letters

Used to start a sentence, as the first letter of proper nouns, for the pronoun _I_, in titles, and to start direct speech.

Colon

Used to introduce additional information.

For example: Use the following:
                eggs, bacon, milk, salt
                and pepper.

Comma

Used as a short pause to separate parts of a sentence and items in a list.

For example: The boy, a great
                athlete, was competing
                in most events.

                I took pens, pencils,
                paper and paints to the
                class.

Dash

Used to provide additional information or show that something is unfinished.

For example: I opened the gift—it
                was just what I
                wanted.

Ellipsis

Used to mark letters or words that have been left out and a pause or interruption

For example: Her birthday party was
                wonderful … the best
                ever!

Exclamation mark

Used to show strong emotion.

For example: That's fantastic news!

Forward slash

Used to show options, shortened forms, in web addresses and instead of _per_, _an_ or _a_.

For example: _true/false_
                _60km/h_

Full stop

Used at the end of a sentence or in some abbreviations.

For example: His birthday was on
                21 Feb.

Hyphen

Used to join words and word parts, clarify meaning and divide words at the end of a line.

For example: _re-signed_ a contract
                brother-in-law
                three-quarters

Parentheses

Used to enclose additional information such as a comment, explanation or example.

For example: Tia (my sister) showed
                me how to use the
                program.

Question mark

Used at the end of a sentence to show a question to be answered.

For example: Did you finish
                everything you wanted
                to?

Quotation marks

Used to indicate direct speech, quotations and specific titles.

For example: 'Did you know the
                Spanish word "siesta"
                means a short nap?'
                Ben asked.

Semicolon

Used to separate short, balanced and linked phrases or clauses. It is stronger than a comma, not as strong as a full stop. It can also be used to separate items in a list of phrases or clauses.

For example: I bought new shoes;
                they were on sale.

                I need 12 pens, pencils
                and rulers; 24 books,
                six erasers and two
                bags.

Abstract noun

A word which describes things that cannot actually be heard, seen, smelt or tasted.

For example: *anger, beauty, danger, jealousy, loyalty, pain*

Active voice

The voice of the verb which shows that the subject of the sentence is performing the action.

For example: Her friend *drove* the car.

The dog *frightened* the child.

Adjective

A describing word used to add meaning to a noun or pronoun.

For example: He wore a *blue* shirt.

The meal was *delicious*.

Adverb

Adds meaning to a verb, adjective or other adverb. It can tell how, where or when.

For example: He worked *carefully*.

Yesterday, they walked to school.

She *finally* finished.

Agreement

Shows that linked words or phrases agree in terms of case, number, gender and person.

For example: *He is* welcome. *They are* welcome.

She tried to write the story *herself*.

Article

A subclass of determiners where *a* and *an* are indefinite and *the* is definitive.

For example: *a* computer, *an* apple, *the* dog

Auxiliary verb

A 'helping' verb that is used in forming tense, mood and voices with other verbs. The verbs *to be*, *to have* and *to do* are often used as auxiliary verbs.

For example: I *was* thinking of you.

He *does* leave his room in a mess.

We *have* seen it.

Clause

A group of words with a subject and its verb.

For example: *She walked to the station.*

Collective noun

A group of persons or things.

For example: a *class* of pupils, a *flock* of sheep, a *herd* of elephants

Command verb (imperative)

A verb used as an order or command.

For example: *Stop* talking so loudly.

Common noun

A word naming general rather than particular things.

For example: *apple, river, table, colour*

Complex sentence

Has a main (independent) clause and at least one subordinate (dependent) clause.

For example: I like swimming before I walk along the beach.

Compound sentence

Has two or more independent clauses with a linking word.

For example: The nurse worked hard and helped the sick child.

Conjunction

A joining word for words, phrases, clauses and sentences.

For example: I ate an apple *and* a pear.

I was tired *but* I had to work *because* the assignment was due.

Connective

A connecting word that tells order and what is coming next.

For example: I'll finish the dishes *first* and *then* watch a film.

Determiner

A word that is used in front of a noun or pronoun to tell something about it.

For example: *a* tiger, *the* tiger, *some* tigers, *both* tigers, *that* tiger, *three* tigers

Direct speech

Exactly what is spoken, enclosed in quotation marks.

For example: *'Are you feeling thirsty?'* she asked.

Double negative

When two negatives are used together, with the effect of cancelling each other so the negative meaning is lost.

For example: She was*n't* doing *nothing*.

He did*n't* get *no* lunch.

Finite verb

A verb that has a subject. A finite verb must be a part of every sentence and agree with its subject.

For example: The ball *rolls*.

The balls *roll*.

Idiom

A phrase that is not meant literally.

For example: *over the moon*

frog in my throat

Indefinite pronoun

A pronoun that refers to people or things generally and not specifically.

For example: *anybody, anything, everybody, everyone, somebody, something*

Indirect speech

Reports, and often alters, direct speech without the use of quotes.

For example: I asked her to be quiet.
She told me she would leave early.

Main (independent) clause

A group of words that can stand alone and make sense without being dependent on any other part of a sentence.

For example: *I decided to go shopping* after I had my lunch.

Modifier

A word or group of words that affect the meaning of another word in some way by giving more information. They might describe, define or make a meaning more precise.

For example: The TV is in the *largest* room.

Bright-eyed and inquisitive, the squirrel searched for food.

Noun

A word that names a person, place, thing, feeling or idea.

For example: doctor, Paris, suitcase, fear, courage

Object

Shows what or whom the verb affects.

For example: They purchased a *house.*

She wore *blue jeans.*

Paragraph

A group of sentences that are about one main idea. The sentences should follow in a logical order.

Passive voice

The voice of the verb which shows that the subject is having an action done to it.

For example: Max *was tickled* by his sister.

She *was surprised* by the visitors.

Person

Text may be written as the first, second or third person and is indicated by the use of pronouns and verbs.

For example: *I* wrote the book.
It must be *yours.*
Did *he* write the book?

Personal pronoun

Used in place of a person.

First person personal pronouns are: *I, me, mine, we, us, ours.*

Second person personal pronouns are: *you, yours.*

Third person personal pronouns are: *he, his, him, she, hers, her, it, its, they, them, theirs.*

Phrase

A group of words in a sentence which does not contain a finite verb.

For example: She walked *towards the house.*

The car crashed *into the tree.*

Possessive pronoun

A pronoun used to show ownership.

For example: That book is *his.*
I think it's *hers.*
I have *mine* here.
It must be *yours.*

Predicate

What is written or said about the subject of a sentence.

For example: The teacher was *tired and hungry.*

The kitchen was *clean and tidy.*

Preposition

Used in front of a noun or pronoun to describe the relationship.

For example: *under* the water, *to* him, *at* the concert, *before* lunch, *around* them

Pronoun

Used in place of a noun to reduce repetition.

For example: Peter is conscientious. *He* works quietly.

Proper noun

Used to specifically name a person or thing.

For example: *Jemma, Antarctica, Sahara Desert*

Relative pronoun

Used to connect or relate one part of a sentence to another.

For example: Here is the house *that* I want to buy.

I met the man *whose* story I had read.

Sentence

A group of words that makes sense on its own. It may have one or more clauses. It must have a finite verb, a capital letter at the start and end in a full stop, question mark or exclamation mark.

For example: *I'll eat breakfast after I've had a shower.*

Simple sentence

A sentence with only one verb (part of the predicate) and one subject.

For example: *I played a game.*

They ate dinner together.

Slang

Words or phrases in common use that are not considered to be part of standard English.

For example: *aggro, dude.*

Statement

A sentence which states a fact.

For example: *We will not be leaving today.*

Subject

The person or thing who is doing the action in a sentence.

For example: *Mrs Green* taught music.

The *football team* won the game with the last kick.

Subordinate (dependent) clause

A group of words that cannot stand alone and make sense. It is dependent on the main clause for its meaning.

For example: I ate everything on the plate *because I was hungry.*

Tense

Verb tenses tell whether the action is happening in the past, present or future.

For example: I *walked*, I *walk*, I *am walking*, I *will walk*.

Verb

An action or state of being word.

For example: She *read* the book.

He *has written* a story.

They *will eat* dinner.

We *thought* about it.

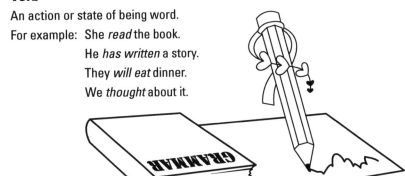

Additional word lists

Words used as prepositions

aboard	among	beyond	in	over	under
about	around	but	inside	past	until
above	at	by	into	per	up
across	before	concerning	like	round	upon
after	behind	despite	near	since	via
against	below	down	of	through	with
along	beneath	during	off	throughout	within
alongside	beside	except	on	till	without
amid	besides	for	onto	to	
amidst	between	from	out	towards	

Prepositional phrases

according to	aside from	behind in	in front of	in regard to	on account of
ahead of	as to	due to	in lieu of	in spite of	on board
apart from	back of	in addition to	in light of	instead of	out of
as far as	because of	in the back of	in place of	in view of	owing to

Words used as adjectives or adverbs

bad	doubtless	fast	loose	right	straight
better	early	first	loud	rough	third
bright	enough	hard	low	second	tight
cheap	even	high	much	sharp	well
close	fair	late	near	slow	worse
deep	far	little	quick	smooth	wrong

There are 19 vowel sounds listed below. Most of these vowel sounds can be written in a number of different ways. The letters used to represent sounds in words are called 'graphemes'.

Knowledge about common graphemes and an understanding of how to use them when selecting the particular one needed to spell a word correctly, are essential spelling skills.

Some of the most commonly used graphemes for each vowel sound are found in the table below.

Sound	Graphemes
'a' as in bat	a (cat)
'a' as in rain	ai (pain) ay (tray) a-e (plate) a (baby) ea (break) ei (rein) ey (grey)
'ar' as in bar	ar (car) a (class) al (calf) au (laugh)
'air' as in pair	air (chair) are (care) ear (bear) ere (there) eir (their)
'aw' as in paw	aw (yawn) or (fork) au (sauce) a (ball) ore (store) oar (roar) oor (poor) ough (fought) augh (caught) al (walk)
'e' as in tell	e (jet) ea (spread)
'ee' as in tree	ee (sheep) ea (beat) y (funny) ie (thief) ei (ceiling) ey (key) i (ski) e-e (athlete)
'er' as in fern	er (germ) ir (girl) ur (purse) or (word) ear (earn) our (journey)
'ear' as in appear	ear (near) eer (deer) ere (here) ier (tier)
'i' as in bit	i (fin) y (pyramid) ui (build)
'i' as in hive	i (find) ie (pie) y (sky) i-e (fine) igh (sigh)
'o' as in top	o (clot) a (wasp) au (sausage) ou (cough)
'o' as in hope	o (no) oa (boat) oe (toe) ow (slow) o-e (home)
'ow' as in cow	ow (down) ou (loud)
'oy' as in toy	oy (boy) oi (coin)
'oo' as in cook	oo (book) u (bush) ou (should)
'oo' as in boot	oo (spoon) ew (flew) ue (true) ou (soup) ui (fruit) o (to)
'u' as in mud	u (truck) o (some) ou (young)
'yu' as in use	u-e (fuse) u (duty) ew (new) ue (avenue) eau (beauty)

There are 25 consonant sounds listed below. Most of these consonant sounds can be written in a number of different ways. The letters used to represent sounds in words are called 'graphemes'.

Knowledge about common graphemes and an understanding of how to use them when selecting the particular one needed to spell a word correctly, are essential spelling skills.

Some of the most commonly used graphemes for each consonant sound are found in the table below.

Sound	Graphemes
'b' as in big	b (bat) bb (rabbit)
'c' as in cat	c (clean) ck (pack) ch (school) k (kite) cc (occupy) que (cheque)
'ch' as in chin	ch (church) tch (watch)
'd' as in dog	d (doll) dd (rudder) ed (talked)
'f' as in fat	f (fed) ff (giraffe) ph (phone) gh (laugh)
'g' as in get	g (goat) gg (egg) gu (guide) gh (ghost)
'h' as in hat	h (have) wh (who)
'j' as in jam	j (jet) g (giant) dge (hedge) gg (suggest)
'l' as in look	l (lot) ll (hill) le (little)
'm' as in met	m (mother) mm (hammer) mb (climb) lm (calm) mn (autumn)
'n' as in now	n (nurse) nn (runner) kn (knot)
'ng' as in sing	ng (strong) n (sink)
'p' as in pot	p (pin) pp (ripped)
'r' as in run	r (red) rr (carry) wr (write)
's' as in sat	s (sun) ss (toss) c (cent) ce (rice) sc (scene)
'sh' as in ship	sh (sheep) s (sugar) ss (pressure) ch (machine) ci (special) ti (station) si (tension)
't' as in tap	t (tent) tt (written) th (Thomas) ed (cooked)
'th' as in thin	th (think)
'th' as in then	th (that) the (breathe)
'v' as in van	v (vase) f (of)
'w' as in was	w (watch) wh (when)
'x' as in box	x (fox) cks (socks)
'y' as in yes	y (yell)
'z' as in zebra	z (zip) zz (fizz) s (has)
'zh' as in measure	s (treasure) si (television)

Prefix	Meaning	Example(s)
anti-	opposed, against	**anti**septic
bi-	two, twice	**bi**cycle
bio-	life	**bio**graphy
circum-	around	**circum**ference
co-	together	**co**operate
contra-	opposite, against	**contra**dict
de-	away, from, down	**de**fer, **de**scend
dis-	apart	**dis**connect
en- em-	make	**en**able, **em**brace
ex-	former	**ex**-premier
for-	not	**for**get
fore-	before	**fore**cast
giga-	billion	**giga**byte
hyper-	over, exclusive	**hyper**active
il-	not	**il**legal
in-	not, in	**in**complete, **in**side
im- ir-	not	**im**possible, **ir**regular
inter-	between, among	**inter**view
mal-	wrong	**mal**function
mega-	million	**mega**byte
micro-	small	**micro**scope
milli-	thousand	**milli**litre
mini-	small	**mini**skirt
mis-	wrongly	**mis**judge
non-	not	**non**sense
out-	outside, detached	**out**patient
post-	after	**post**graduate
pre-	before	**pre**heat
re-	again, back	**re**peat, **re**turn
semi-	half	**semi**circle
sub-	under	**sub**marine
super-	over, above	**super**human
trans-	across	**trans**port
tri-	three, triple	**tri**cycle
un-	not	**un**done
uni-	one, single	**uni**form
with-	against, away	**with**hold

Suffix	Meaning	Example(s)
-able, -ible	capable of, for	adapt**able**, poss**ible**
-al, -ical	of, relating to	matern**al**, mag**ical**
-ar	like	circul**ar**
-ate	to make	aggrav**ate**
-ation	act of	invit**ation**
-dom	state of	free**dom**
-er, -or	one who	farm**er**, act**or**
-ess	feminine of nouns	princ**ess**
-fold	number of parts, times	two**fold**
-ful	able to, full of	help**ful**, plate**ful**
-ion	action, state, quality	considerat**ion**, promot**ion**
-ise	make into	human**ise**
-ish	belonging, like	girl**ish**, Swed**ish**
-ism	state, quality, act of	hero**ism**, bapt**ism**
-ist	one who	art**ist**
-ive	like, connected with	nat**ive**, protect**ive**
-less	without	child**less**
-ly	like, how, when	man**ly**, dark**ly**, year**ly**
-ment	result, state, quality of	achieve**ment**, judg**ment**
-ous	full of	nerv**ous**
-phobia	fear, dread	claustro**phobia**

LATIN ROOT WORDS

Root word	Meaning	Example(s)
scribe	writing	de**scribe**, in**scribe**, **scrib**ble, pre**scribe**, tran**scribe**
port	carry	trans**port**, **port**able, re**port**, ex**port**, im**port**, sup**port**
ped	foot	**ped**estrian, **ped**al, **ped**estal, im**ped**e, ex**ped**ition
spire	breathe	in**spire**, con**spire**, re**spire**, tran**spire**
mit	send, let go	trans**mit**, o**mit**, ad**mit**, per**mit**, re**mit**
fact	make, do	manu**fact**ure, **fact**or, **fact**ion, satis**fact**ion, **fact**ory
duce, duct	to lead	con**duct**, intro**duce**, pro**duce**, e**duc**ate, con**duct**or
capit	head	**capit**al, **cap**tain, de**capit**ate, **capit**ulate
flu	flow	**flu**id, **flu**ent, in**flu**ence, af**flu**ent, ef**flu**ent
manu	hand	**manu**al, **manu**facture, **manu**script, **man**ipulate
aqua, aque	water	**aqua**tic, **aqua**rium, **aqua**plane, **aqu**educt, **Aqua**rius
aud	hear	**aud**io, **aud**ience, **aud**ible, **aud**ition
annu	year	**annu**al, **ann**iversary, bi**annu**al, **annu**ity
bene	well	**bene**fit, **bene**ficial, **bene**factor, **bene**ficiary, **bene**volent
prem, prim	first	**prim**ary, **prim**e, **prim**itive, **prim**er, **prem**ier
unus	one	**un**it
duo	two	**du**et
tres	three	**tri**angle
quatuor	four	**qua**rter
quinque	five	**quin**tet
sex	six	**sex**tuplet
septum	seven	**Sept**ember (7th month on Roman calendar)
octo	eight	**octo**pus
novem	nine	**Novem**ber (9th month on Roman calendar)
decem	ten	**dec**imal
centum	hundred	**centu**ry
mille	thousand	**milli**metre

GREEK ROOT WORDS

Root word	Meaning	Example(s)
meter, metre	measure	centi**metre**, milli**metre**, thermo**meter**, baro**meter**, pedo**meter**, speedo**meter**
micro	small	**micro**scopic, **micro**scope, **micro**phone
aero	air	**aero**naut, **aer**ate, **aero**plane, **aer**ial
sphere	globe, ball	atmo**sphere**, strato**sphere**, hemi**sphere**
tele	far off	**tele**phone, **tele**port, **tele**vise, **tele**vision
logy	word, knowledge, science of	psycho**logy**, bio**logy**, zoo**logy**, neuro**logy**
auto	self	**auto**matic, **auto**biography, **auto**graph, **auto**mobile
logos	word, reason	**log**ic, **log**istic, **log**ical

LIST 1

about	choose	friend	none	their
ache	colour	guess	ocean	though
address	coming	half	often	through
afraid	cough	heard	once	together
again	could	hospital	people	tomorrow
agree	country	hour	picture	tonight
almost	couple	hungry	piece	touch
always	cousin	important	please	trouble
among	daughter	insect	promise	Tuesday
answer	decide	instead	question	uncle
any	definite	interesting	quick	used
around	different	invite	ready	useful
August	difficult	January	reason	vegetable
aunt	discuss	knew	remember	voice
autumn	doctor	know	rough	Wednesday
balloon	does	lately	said	welcome
beautiful	don't	laugh	separate	where
because	done	library	September	which
been	during	listen	sign	who
beginning	early	lose	since	women
behaviour	easy	making	some	won't
bicycle	eight	many	someone	would
breakfast	every	meant	special	write
built	exercise	message	spread	writing
business	famous	might	straight	wrong
busy	February	minute	strange	wrote
buy	finish	naughty	sure	yesterday
careful	forgotten	nearly	surprise	

LIST 2

accident	customer	incident	private
adventure	damage	information	procedure
aeroplane	decoration	injury	punishment
altogether	delicious	instrument	pure
ambulance	disappointing	intelligent	pyjamas
amusing	discovery	jealous	quantity
anxious	disgraceful	knowledge	reasonable
appear	distract	lawyer	recreation
appreciate	division	league	religion
argument	doubt	machine	repair
assembly	election	material	request
association	electric	medicine	scarce
athlete	enormous	migrate	separate
attendance	enough	multiplication	serious
audience	excitement	museum	silence
author	extreme	musical	skilful
automatic	failure	mystery	subtraction
avenue	fashion	necessary	support
awful	favourite	neighbour	surround
balance	finally	nephew	technology
believe	forty	nervous	unknown
careless	frequent	niece	valuable
celebrate	generous	opinion	variety
centre	gradual	oxygen	visitor
certain	heritage	parliament	weary
chocolate	hesitate	passenger	weight
comfortable	honest	permission	weird
committee	horrible	persuade	yacht
conversation	imagination	physical	youth
curtain	immediately	population	

LIST 3

accessories	convenient	foreigner	irrelevant	outrageous	silhouette
acquaintance	cooperate	fortunately	irreplaceable	paralyse	sincerely
acquire	courageous	freight	irresponsible	participant	sophisticated
admittance	curious	fugitive	itinerary	permitted	spaghetti
adolescence	deceased	furious	jewellery	phenomenon	spontaneous
anniversary	definite	gauge	kidnapped	pneumonia	statistics
anonymous	desperate	genuine	knowledgeable	politician	successful
appalling	diabetes	glamorous	labelled	possession	sufficient
Arctic	diarrhoea	government	legendary	possibility	supervisor
assistance	difference	grammar	limousine	professional	surgeon
asthmatic	disappearance	grieve	maintenance	pronunciation	suspicious
basically	disapproval	guarantee	manageable	prosecute	technique
bouquet	disastrous	guard	manually	protein	therapeutic
boutique	discipline	hallucination	millionaire	questionnaire	tragedy
bureau	discrimination	harass	miraculous	queue	transferred
campaign	discussion	hereditary	mortgage	reassurance	twelfth
casualty	disease	hilarious	muscle	rebellious	unanimous
cautious	disinfectant	humorous	mysterious	receipt	unconscious
cemetery	distinguish	hypothetical	nausea	recommend	unique
chauffeur	documentary	hysterical	negotiate	referee	unnecessary
choreography	economically	ignorance	numerous	regretted	vaccinate
coincidence	efficient	illiterate	nutritious	rehabilitation	vague
colleague	eightieth	imaginative	obedient	relevant	visibility
commercial	electrician	immaculate	obese	responsibility	volunteered
commitment	embarrass	inappropriate	obscene	restaurant	vulnerable
communicate	encourage	independence	obsessive	resuscitate	wintry
competitive	escalator	indigenous	occasion	rhythm	worshipped
concussion	essential	ineligible	occurred	rumour	
congratulations	eventually	ingredient	offence	satellite	
conscientious	fascinate	inseparable	omitted	schedule	
conscious	fatigue	intermediate	opportunity	siege	
controversial	fierce	interrupt	ordinary	significant	

LIST 1

Words	Examples
angel/angle	We put the angel on the Christmas tree. A triangle might have a right angle.
as/like	I did as I was told. I was like my sister.
ate/eaten	I ate breakfast. I have eaten breakfast.
beat/beaten	We will beat them. We should have beaten them.
became/become	She became a star. She will become a star.
began/begun	He began the work. He has begun to work.
been/being	I have been to school. I like being at school.
beside/besides	I stood beside him. Who, besides your dad, is home?
blew/blown	The wind blew. The papers have blown away.
breath/breathe	He took a deep breath. He can breathe deeply.
can/may/might	She can do that. May I do that? I may do that. I might be able to do that.
came/come	She came late. They will come later.
chose/choose	I chose the apple. I will choose an apple.
dairy/diary	The milk came from the dairy. He wrote in his diary.
desert/dessert	The desert was dry. He deserted them. We had ice-cream for dessert.
did/done	He did the work. He has done the work.
forgot/forgotten	She forgot the number. He has forgotten to bring it.
gave/give	She gave me the book. I will give you the book.
gone/went	He has gone to school. She went to school.
hid/hidden	Mum hid the Christmas presents. The presents were hidden from us.
its/it's	The dog is wagging its tail. It's a sunny day.
knew/know/known	I knew the teacher. I know who she is. I wish I had known before.
laid/lain	It was laid on the table. It had lain on the table for a while.
learn/teach	I had to learn the words. She can teach me how to do it.
lend/borrow	I will lend you the book. May I borrow the book?
loose/lose	These trousers feel loose. Don't lose your phone.
meter/metre	The meter was running. It was a metre long.
of/off	I was tired of working. I took off my hat.
outdoor/outdoors	Cricket is an outdoor sport. We played it outdoors.
passed/past	I passed the test. I walked past her.
practice/practise	He is going to football practice. He will practise his skills.
principal/principle	She is the principal of the school. She followed a basic principle.
quiet/quite	I was very quiet. It was quite funny.
rapt/wrapped	I was rapt with the result. I wrapped a present.
risen/rose	The sun had risen before I woke. The sun rose before I did.
role/roll	She played the role of a doctor. She ate a salad roll for lunch.
showed/shown	I showed her where I lived. He has shown me the way to go.
storey/story	They lived on the top storey of the building. I read the story.
their/there/they're	That is their house. They live there. They're going out.
threw/through	I threw the ball. I walked through the room.
tore/torn	He tore the shirt he was wearing. The shirt is torn.
wear/where/we're	I will wear the dress. Where are you? We're going to school.
went/gone	They went an hour ago. They have already gone.
who/which	I have two brothers who are older. I have two kittens which are cute.
who's/whose	Who's leaving now? Do you know whose dog it is?

LIST 2

Rootword	Example(s)
accept/except	Please accept this gift. Everyone went except Drew.
addition/edition	I completed the addition problems. There is a new edition of that book.
advice/advise	She asked for my advice. I would advise you to finish it.
affect/effect	She was affected by the news. It had a good effect on her.
amend/emend	They should amend the rule. He needs to emend (edit) his work.
ballet/ballot	Her ballet dress was beautiful. We needed a ballot paper to vote.
belief/believe	My belief is that you will do well. I believe you will win.
charted/chartered	He charted the data. He chartered a boat for the day.
continual/continuous	She was in continual pain. It was a continuous line.
councillor/counsellor	The local councillor approved the plans. The counsellor listened to her.
dependant/dependent	The woman had two dependants. The child was dependent on her mother.
device/devise	The electronic device was expensive. She had to devise a new plan.
elicit/illicit	He tried to elicit information. The drug was illicit.
eligible/legible	The school was eligible for the grant. Her writing was legible.
emigrant/immigrant	The emigrant left his country. The immigrant arrived in his new country.
emission/omission	There was a gas emission. The omission of her name was an oversight.
employee/employer	The new employee worked hard. The boss was their employer.
forgave/forgiven	I easily forgave my best friend. I told her she was forgiven.
formally/formerly	I was dressed formally. I was formerly at another address.
human/humane	He is a human being. They had to treat the animal in a humane way.
licence/license	He had a driver's licence. He had to license the car.
mediate/meditate	She had to mediate between the groups. I took time to meditate and relax.
mistaken/mistook	I was mistaken about the time. I mistook the time it would take.
overtaken/overtook	They had overtaken the slow car. They overtook the car.
premier/premiere	The premier is the state leader. We went to the film premiere.
proof/prove	You need the right proof first. You will have to prove it's true.
refuge/refugee	He took refuge from the storm. The refugee arrived from another country.
review/revue	Write a review of the book. The musical revue was very funny.
scared/scarred	I was scared of the dark. The burn scarred my skin.
scraped/scrapped	She scraped her knee when she fell. I scrapped the work I was doing.
stationary/stationery	The train was stationary. The stationery included pencils.
suit/suite	He wore the new suit to the party. We stayed in an expensive hotel suite.
summary/summery	The summary was very brief. It was a fine, summery day.

Answers

1. **The following illustrations should be coloured.**

   (a) ball bat bed book $\boxed{\text{b}}$

   (b) car can cat cross $\boxed{\text{c}}$

   (c) dog door dress dinosaur $\boxed{\text{d}}$

   (d) tree tap tiger table $\boxed{\text{t}}$

   (e) sun seal star stamp $\boxed{\text{s}}$

1. Colour the pictures with the same first sound. Write the sound in the box.

(a)

(b)

(c)

(d)

(e)

PUPIL NAME

Answers

1. Teacher check

2. (a) bed   (b) car   (c) dog

    (d) six   (e) cat   (f) book

    (g) ten   (h) rat

3. Answers will vary.

1. Circle the first letter of each word. Write the word.

(a) you _____

(b) day _____

(c) look _____

(d) me _____

(e) sit _____

(f) has _____

(g) end _____

(h) yes _____

2. Write the first letter for each word.

(a) _____ed

(b) _____ar

(c) _____og

(d) _____ix

(e) _____at

(f) _____ook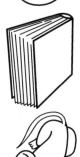

(g) _____en

(h) _____at

3. Write a word that starts with each letter.

(a) a _____

(b) e _____

(c) i _____

(d) o _____

(e) u _____

(f) t _____

(g) w _____

(h) g _____

(i) b _____

(j) r _____

Answers

1. **The following illustrations should be coloured.**

   (a) cat rat mat hat   [t]

   (b) man can fan pan   [n]

   (c) bag flag rag tag   [g]

   (d) car bar jar star   [r]

   (e) bus cross dress grass [s]

1. Colour the pictures with the same last sound. Write the sound in the box.

PUPIL NAME

(a)

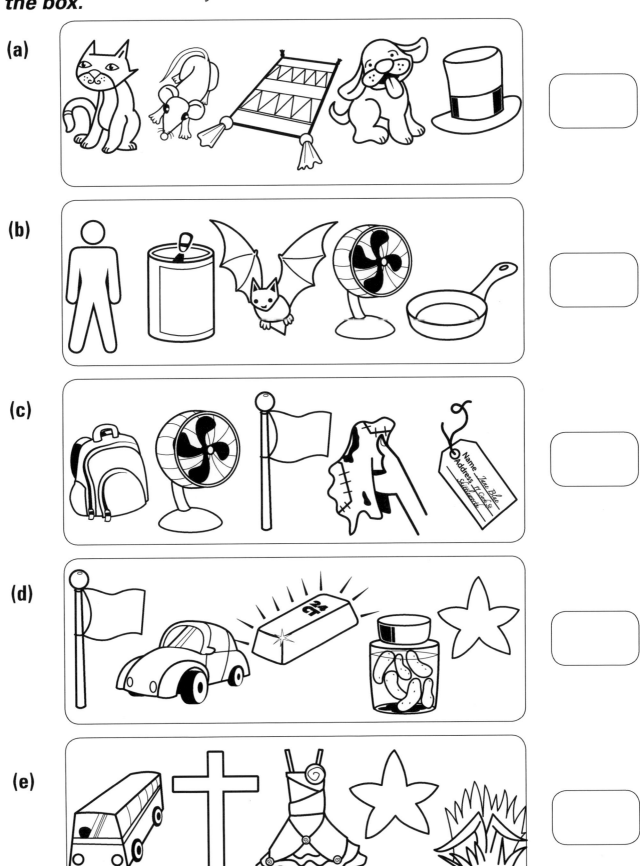

(b)

(c)

(d)

(e)

Answers

1. Teacher check

2. (a) mop   (b) mat   (c) bat

    (d) milk   (e) belt   (f) flag

    (g) bell   (h) seven

3. Answers will vary.

1. Circle the last letter of each word. Write the word.

(a) red _____

(b) ten _____

(c) for _____

(d) wet _____

(e) puff _____

(f) mum _____

(g) cow _____

(h) pink _____

2. Write the last letter for each word.

(a) mo_____

(b) ma_____

(c) ba_____

(d) mil_____

(e) bel_____

(f) fla_____

(g) bel_____

(h) seve_____

3. Write a word that ends with each letter.

(a) _____ n

(b) _____ s

(c) _____ m

(d) _____ b

(e) _____ g

(f) _____ x

(g) _____ o

(h) _____ p

(i) _____ d

(j) _____ t

PUPIL NAME

Answers

1. **The following illustrations should be coloured.**

   (a) pen bed jet ten | e |

   (b) dog mop rock log | o |

   (c) car cat hat fan | a |

   (d) sun duck bus sum | u |

   (e) bin pig pin fin | i |

1. Colour the pictures with the same middle sound. Write the sound in the box.

(a)

(b)

(c)

(d)

(e)

PUPIL NAME

Answers

1. **Teacher check**

2. (a) duck   (b) ring   (c) pin

    (d) crisp   (e) stamp   (f) rock

    (g) kiss   (h) crack

3. (a) bin   (b) dog   (c) ant

    (d) fan   (e) pen   (f) arm

    (g) cup   (h) cat

1. Circle the middle letter of each word. Write the word.

(a) had _____   (b) did _____

(c) can _____   (d) big _____

(e) bed _____   (f) and _____

(g) dad _____   (h) get _____

2. Write the middle letter for each word.

(a) d____ck   (b) r____ng

(c) p____n   (d) cr____sp

(e) st____mp    (f) r____ck

(g) k____ss   (h) cr____ck

3. Write a word with each middle letter.

(a) ____i____   (b) ____o____

(c) ____n____   (d) ____a____

(e) ____e____   (f) ____r____

(g) ____u____    (h) ____a____

Answers

1. Teacher check

2. (a) blanket   (b) blind   (c) blow

3. (a) clap   (b) club   (c) cliff   (d) clock

4. Circled words:

   (a) clap

   (b) clock, blink

   (c) classroom, clean

   (d) blue

   (e) black, blonde

   (f) blunt

   (g) clown

   (h) blank

1. Circle bl in each word.

(a) blob   (b) blue   (c) black

(d) blink   (e) blank   (f) bleed

2. Write bl to finish the words.

(a) _____anket   (b) _____ind   (c) _____ow

3. Write cl to finish the words.

(a) _____ap   (b) _____ub

(c) _____iff   (d) _____ock

4. Circle the bl and cl words. Write yes or no.

(a) Can you clap?   _____

(b) Can a clock blink?   _____

(c) Is the classroom clean?   _____

(d) Is the sky blue?   _____

(e) Is your hair black or blonde? _____

(f) Is your pencil blunt?   _____

(g) Is a clown funny?   _____

(h) Is this page blank?   _____

PUPIL NAME

Answers

1. Picture order is: flame, float, flag, floor, flea.

2. Picture order is: globe, glove, glow, glass, glue.

3. (a) fly

   (b) flip

   (c) floss

   (d) glass

   (e) flat

   (f) flap

1. Circle the fl in each word. Match the word to the picture.

flag	flame	floor	flea	float

2. Circle the gl in each word. Match the word to the picture.

glass	glue	glove	globe	glow

3. Choose the right word. Draw a picture.

(a) The bird can | fly | float |.

(b) I can | flop | flip | a coin.

(c) I can | floss | gloss | my teeth.

(d) I can drink from a | glove | glass |.

(e) The page is | flat | gold |.

(f) The cat went out the door | fluff | flap |.

Answers

1. (a) play   (b) plane   (c) plant   (d) plank

2. (a) plant

    (b) plane

    (c) plank

    (d) play

3. (a) sleep   (b) sleeve   (c) sling   (d) slide

4. slip, slop, slap

5. Teacher check

1. Write *pl* to finish the words.

(a) _____ay (b)_____ane (c)_____ant (d)_____ank

2. Write the missing *pl* word.

(a) The green _____ grows in the garden.

(b) I saw the _____ high in the sky.

(c) The _____ was made of wood.

(d) I like to _____ games.

3. Write *sl* to finish the words.

(a) _____eep (b)_____eeve (c)_____ing (d)_____ide

4. In summer we should

_____ip, _____op, _____ap.

5. Draw two friends playing on a slide and a dog sleeping.

Answers

1. (a) swan   (b) swamp   (c) swim

    (d) swing   (e) sweep

2. (a) twinkle   (b) twig   (c) twins

    (d) twenty   (e) twist

3. (a) tweet   (b) swing

PUPIL NAME

1. Circle the *sw* in each word. Write the word under the picture.

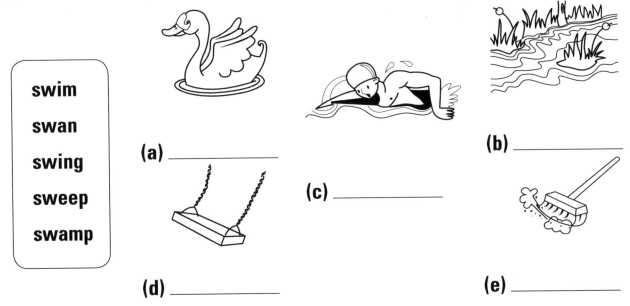

swim

swan

swing

sweep

swamp

(a) _____

(b) _____

(c) _____

(d) _____

(e) _____

2. Circle the *tw* in each word. Write the word under the picture.

twig

twins

twinkle

twenty

twist

(a) _____

(b) _____

(c) _____

(d) _____

(e) _____

3. Choose the right word. Draw a picture.

(a) A bird can | tweet | twist |.

(b) There is a | switch | swing | to play on.

Answers

1. (a) crab   (b) crow   (c) crown   (d) cross

2. (a) crayon

   (b) cry

   (c) crack

   (d) cream

3. (a) drip   (b) dragon   (c) drink   (d) dress

4. Circled words:

   (a) drink

   (b) dream

   (c) draw

   (d) drive

   (e) dry

   (f) drop

Answer to questions will vary.

1. Write cr to finish the words.

(a) _____ab   (b) _____ow   (c) _____own   (d) _____oss

2. Write the missing cr word.

(a) I can draw with a _____.

(b) I will _____ if I am sad.

(c) The cup has a _____.

(d) I like ice- _____.

cream

crack

crayon

cry

3. Write dr to finish the words.

(a) _____ip   (b) _____agon   (c) _____ink   (d) _____ess

4. Circle the dr words. Write yes or no.

(a) Do you drink milk?   _____

(b) Have you had a dream?   _____

(c) Can you draw?   _____

(d) Do you drive a car?   _____

(e) Is your hair dry?   _____

(f) Can you drop a ball?   _____

Answers

1. Pictures match – trumpet, tree, trunk, train, tray

2. (a) trap   (b) trip   (c) trim

   (d) try   (e) trot   (f) trick

3. Pictures match – sky, skull, skates, skip, skis

4. (a) skin

   (b) skid

   (c) skunk

5. Teacher check

PUPIL NAME

1. Circle the *tr* in each word. Match the word to the picture.

tree   train   tray   trumpet   trunk

2. Write *tr* to finish the words.

(a) _____ap   (b) _____ip   (c) _____im

(d) _____y   (e) _____ot   (f) _____ick

3. Circle the *sk* in each word. Match the word to the picture.

skip   skis   sky   skull   skates

4. Write the missing word.

(a) My _____ feels cold.

(b) The car did a _____ .

(c) A _____ is an animal.

> *skid*
>
> *skunk*
>
> *skin*

5. Draw two girls skipping next to a skinny tree.

Answers

1. (a) spider   (b) speak   (c) spoon

    (d) spot   (e) spill

2. (a) string   (b) stew   (c) street

    (d) stem   (e) star

3. Circled words:

    (a) spider, spell

    (b) stick, splash

    (c) stone, stay, still

    (d) stew, steak

    (e) stop, step

    Answers will vary.

1. Circle the *sp* in each word. Write the word under the picture.

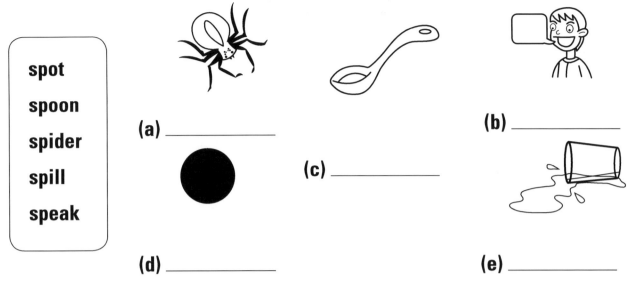

spot

spoon

spider

spill

speak

(a) _____

(b) _____

(c) _____

(d) _____

(e) _____

2. Circle the *st* in each word. Write the word under the picture.

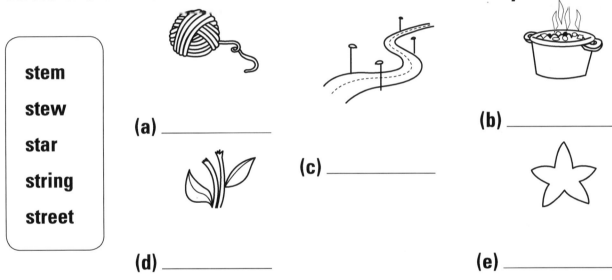

stem

stew

star

string

street

(a) _____

(b) _____

(c) _____

(d) _____

(e) _____

3. Circle the *sp* and *st* words. Write yes or no.

(a) Can a spider spell?   _____

(b) Can a stick make a splash?   _____

(c) Can a stone stay still?   _____

(d) Do you eat stew and steak? _____

(e) Can you stop on a step?   _____

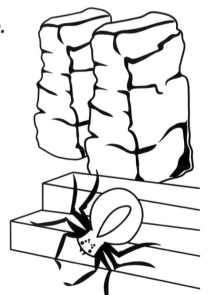

Answers·

1. (a) sent   (b) rent   (c) cent

   (d) dent   (e) tent   (f) bent

   (g) vent   (h) lent

2. (a) tent

   (b) sent

   (c) dent

   (d) went

   (e) rent

3. (a) left   (b) lift   (c) soft

   (d) sift   (e) raft   (f) craft

   (g) drift   (h) swift

4. (a) raft, drift

   (b) left

   (c) lift, soft

   (d) craft

Answers to questions will vary.

1. Finish the words so they all rhyme with *went*.

(a) se_____ (b) re_____ (c) ce_____ (d) de_____

(e) te_____ (f) be_____ (g) ve_____ (h) le_____

2. Use a word with *nt* to finish the sentence.

(a) We slept in a _____.

(b) I _____ a letter.

(c) The car had a _____ in its door.

(d) She _____ to the shop.

(e) He had to pay the _____.

3. Write *ft* to end each word.

(a) le_____ (b) li_____ (c) so_____ (d) si_____

(e) ra_____ (f) cra_____ (g) dri_____ (h) swi_____

4. Put a line under the *ft* words. Write yes or no.

(a) Can a raft drift? _____

(b) Do you draw with your left hand? _____

(c) Can you lift a soft toy? _____

(d) Do you like art and craft? _____

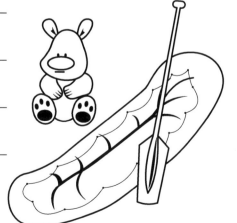

Answers

1. (a) best   (b) rest   (c) nest

   (d) test   (e) last   (f) mast

   (g) fast   (h) blast

2. (a) first

   (b) must

3. (a) belt   (b) melt   (c) felt   (d) bolt

4. (a) kept   (b) wept   (c) crept   (d) slept

5. (a) rest, slept

   (b) melt

   (c) kept, belt

   (d) crept, nest

Teacher check drawings.

1. Write *st* to finish the rhyming words.

(a) be_____ (b) re_____ (c) ne_____ (d) te_____

(e) la_____ (f) ma_____ (g) fa_____ (h) bla_____

2. Choose the right word.

(a) He came [first | lost] in the race.

(b) She [just | must] sit down.

3. Write *lt* to finish the words.

(a) be_____ (b) me_____ (c) fe_____ (d) bo_____

4. Write *pt* to finish the words.

(a) ke_____ (b) we_____ (c) cre_____ (d) sle_____

5. Put a line under the words that end in *st, lt* or *pt*. **Draw a picture.**

(a) I had a rest when I slept on the sofa.

(b) The ice-cream will melt in the sun.

(c) He kept the belt on the chair.

(d) He crept over to see the nest.

PUPIL NAME

Answers

1. **Rhyming words are circled.**

   (end)   (bend)   send   band

   kind   pond   (mend)   (lend)

2. **Rhyming words are circled.**

   (cold)   (gold)   (fold)   held

   (sold)   (told)   (bold)   (hold)

3. (a) send

   (b) gold

   (c) cold

   (d) find

   (e) told

   (f) band

   (g) kind

   (h) hold

1. Write nd to finish the words. Circle the words that rhyme.

end   be_____   se_____   ba_____

ki_____   po_____   me_____   le_____

2. Write ld to finish the words. Put a tick next to the words that rhyme.

cold ☐   go_____ ☐

fo_____ ☐   he_____ ☐

so_____ ☐   to ☐

bo_____ ☐   ho_____ ☐

3. Colour the right word.

(a) Did she | send | bend | the letter?

(b) My mum has a | sold | gold | ring.

(c) My hands feel | cold | bold |.

(d) I want to | find | mind | the lost dog.

(e) He | fold | told | her to sit down.

(f) The | sand | band | played a song.

(g) The teacher is | kind | mind |.

(h) I can | hold | sold | the cup.

Answers

1. (a) camp   (b) ramp   (c) bump

   (d) lump   (e) lamp   (f) stamp

   (g) dump   (h) jump

2. Circled words:

   (a) stamp

   (b) camp

   (c) jump

   (d) lump

   (e) damp

   (f) lamp

   Answers to questions will vary.

3. milk, walk

4. (a) talk   (b) sulk   (c) hulk

   (d) bulk   (e) milk   (f) walk

PUPIL NAME

1. Write *mp* to finish the words.

(a) ca_____   (b) ra_____   (c) bu_____   (d) lu_____

(e) la_____   (f) sta_____   (g) du_____   (h) ju_____

2. Circle the *mp* words. Write yes or no.

(a) Can you stamp your foot?   _____

(b) Have you been on a camp?   _____

(c) Can you jump high?   _____

(d) Is there a lump on your nose?   _____

(e) Is your hair damp?   _____

(f) Can you turn on a lamp?   _____

3. Circle the *lk* words. Draw a picture.

I like to drink milk.	I can walk to school.

4. Write *lk* to finish the words.

(a) ta_____   (b) su_____   (c) hu_____

(d) bu_____   (e) mi_____   (f) wa_____

Answers

1. (a) tank   (b) wink   (c) sink
   (d) link   (e) bank

2. (a) rink
   (b) pink
   (c) sank

3. (a) tusk   (b) dusk   (c) mask
   (d) desk   (e) ask

4. (a) rusk
   (b) desk

PUPIL NAME

1. Circle the nk in each word. Write the word under the picture.

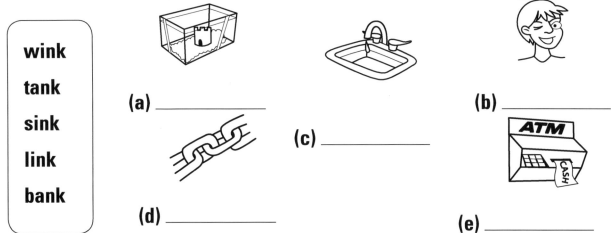

wink
tank
sink
link
bank

(a) _____

(b) _____

(c) _____

(d) _____

(e) _____

2. Choose the right word. Draw a picture.

(a) I like to skate at the ice | rink | ink |.

(b) The dress is | drink | pink |.

(c) The small boat | sank | blank |.

3. Circle the sk in each word. Write the word under the picture.

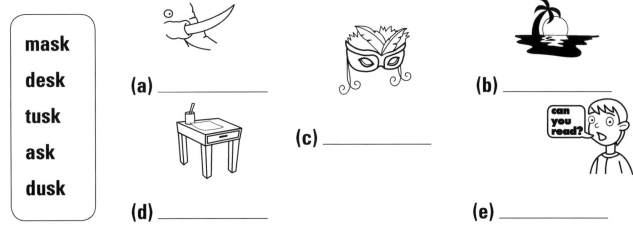

mask
desk
tusk
ask
dusk

(a) _____

(b) _____

(c) _____

(d) _____

(e) _____

4. Choose the right word. Draw a picture.

(a) The baby had a | rusk | tusk | to eat.

(b) She sat at the | task | desk |.

Answers

1.

hill	fill
will	still
bill	pill

fall	hall
call	tall
ball	small

2. (a) cuff   (b) huff   (c) puff

    (d) fluff   (e) stuff   (f) scruff

3. (a) boss   (b) cross   (c) toss

    (d) loss   (e) floss   (f) moss

4. Teacher check

5. (a) full

    (b) toss

    (c) cross

    (d) stuff

    (e) hill, puff

PUPIL NAME

1. Write *ll* to finish the rhyming words.

hi_____   fi_____

wi_____   sti_____

bi_____   pi_____

fa_____   ha_____

ca_____   ta_____

ba_____   sma_____

2. Write *ff* to finish the rhyming words.

(a) cu_____   (b) hu_____   (c) pu_____

(d) flu_____   (e) stu_____   (f) scru_____

3. Write *ss* to finish the rhyming words.

(a) bo_____   (b) cro_____   (c) to_____

(d) lo_____   (e) flo_____   (f) mo_____

4. Read and draw.

A small doll with a red dress.	A wolf who can huff and puff.

5. Choose the right word.

(a) The glass is [full | fall].

(b) He will [fuss | toss] the ball.

(c) The teacher is [cross | floss].

(d) There is [stiff | stuff] on the bed.

(e) I can walk up a [still | hill] and not [puff | off].

Answers·

1. Teacher check

2. (a) bunch (b) branch (c) pinch

3. (a) such

   (b) chop

   (c) rich

   (d) chick

   (e) chair

1. Circle the *ch* sound. Draw a picture for the word.

chip	chin	chop	rich
chat	chair	bench	church

2. Write the word that rhymes.

lunch

ranch

finch

(a) b_____ (b) b_____ (c) p_____

3. Choose the right word.

(a) It was | such | much | a nice day.

(b) He can | chip | chop | the wood.

(c) The | rich | chin | man had a new car.

(d) The small | chick | chat | is yellow.

(e) I will sit on my | chimp | chair |.

Answers

1. (a) shed   (b) ship   (c) fish   (d) rash

2. (a) she   (b) shin   (c) shut   (d) shop

3. Teacher check

4. (a) cash

    (b) rush

    (c) shed

    (d) fish

    (e) ship

    (f) wish

Answers to questions will vary.

1. Write *sh* to finish the words. Draw a picture.

(a) _____ed   (b) _____ip   (c) fi_____   (d) ra_____

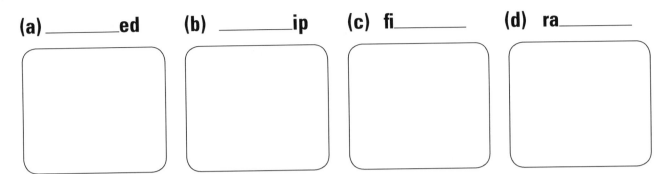

2. Write the *sh* word that rhymes.

(a) he _____   (b) bin _____

(c) but _____   (d) hop _____

shut   she

shop   shin

3. Read and draw.

| She went to the shop. It was shut. | He had a gash on his shin. |

4. Circle the *sh* words. Write yes or no.

(a) Do you have lots of cash?   _____

(b) Are you always in a rush?   _____

(c) Does your house have a shed?   _____

(d) Do you like to eat fish?   _____

(e) Have you been on a ship?   _____

(f) Can you make a wish?   _____

PUPIL NAME

TEACHER INFORMATION

As the focus of this page is spelling, both pronunciations of the digraph *th* have been included and not differentiated; for example: *th*in (unvoiced), *th*at (voiced). Some teachers may wish to discuss this difference with their students.

Answers

1. Picture order is: moth, thumb, thin, bath.

2. (a) the   (b) that   (c) them   (d) thing

   (e) thick   (f) with   (g) both   (h) path

   (i) three   (j) teeth   (k) think   (l) than

3. (a) thick   (b) that   (c) think   (d) three

4. (a) bath

   (b) thank

   (c) throw

   (d) moth

   (e) think, three

   (f) thaw

   Answers to the questions will vary.

1. Circle the *th* sound. Write the word under the picture.

| bath | moth | thin | thumb |

_____   _____   _____   _____

2. Write *th* to finish the word.

(a) _____e   (b) _____at   (c) _____em   (d) _____ing

(e) _____ick   (f) wi_____   (g) bo_____   (h) pa_____

(i) _____ree   (j) tee_____   (k) _____ink   (l) _____an

3. Write the *th* word that rhymes.

(a) brick _____   (b) hat _____

(c) pink _____   (d) tree _____

 *that*    *think*    *three*    *thick*

4. Circle the *th* words. Write yes or no.

(a) Have you ever had a bath? _____

(b) Do you say thank you? _____

(c) Can you throw a ball? _____

(d) Can a moth draw? _____

(e) Can you think of three words? _____

(f) Can ice thaw?

PUPIL NAME

I	_____	am	_____
go	_____	if	_____
is	_____	it	_____
me	_____	my	_____
of	_____	on	_____
to	_____	up	_____
we	_____	at	_____
in	_____	no	_____
and	_____	big	_____
bed	_____	cat	_____

PUPIL NAME

can	_____	car	_____
day	_____	did	_____
end	_____	had	_____
has	_____	sit	_____
the	_____	top	_____
see	_____	was	_____
wet	_____	yes	_____
you	_____	look	_____
dog	_____	get	_____
mum	_____	dad	_____

Answers

1. if, is, it

2. and, bed, did, end, had

3. can, car, day, had, has, was

4. (a) Is the desk red?

   (b) Can you read a book?

   (c) She has a new pencil.

   (d) Can you see the sun?

   (e) He was six years old.

5. Answers will vary.

6. (a) see   (b) had   (c) to, you   (d) my

1. Write the words that begin with *i.*

_____ _____ _____

2. Write the words that end with *d* .

_____ _____ _____

_____ _____

3. Write the words that have *a* **in the middle.**

_____ _____ _____

_____ _____ _____

and	*bed*
can	*car*
day	*did*
end	*had*
has	*if*
is	*it*
my	*see*
the	*to*
was	*you*

4. Which word is not spelt correctly? Circle it. Write the word correctly.

(a) Is th desk red? _____

(b) Can yu read a book? _____

(c) She haz a new pencil. _____

(d) Can you seee the sun? _____

(e) He wos six years old. _____

5. Use three list words in a sentence.

_____

6. Write a list word that rhymes with:

(a) be _____   (b) bad _____

(c) do _____   (d) sky _____

PUPIL NAME

Answers

1. (a) an   (b) an   (c) as   (d) it

   (e) he   (f) to   (g) as   (h) we

   (i) he   (j) do

2. (a) cat   (b) bat   (c) sat   (d) fat

   Teacher check pictures.

3. (a) bin   (b) win   (c) spin   (d) pink

   Teacher check pictures.

4. (a) ran   (b) fan   (c) band   (d) stand

   Teacher check pictures.

1. Write the small word in each word.

(a) and _____

(b) can _____

(c) has _____

(d) sit _____

(e) the _____

(f) top _____

(g) was _____

(h) wet _____

(i) she _____

(j) dog _____

2. Add *at* to finish each word. Draw a picture.

(a) c_____

(b) b_____

(c) s_____

(d) f_____

3. Add *in* to finish each word. Draw a picture.

(a) b_____

(b) w_____

(c) sp_____

(d) p_____k

4. Add *an* to finish each word. Draw a picture.

(a) r_____

(b) f_____

(c) b_____d

(d) st_____d

Answers

1. (a) am

   (b) and

   (c) bed

   (d) on

   (e) big

2. (a) can, has, to   (1, 2, 3)

   (b) end, me, yes   (1, 3, 2)

   (c) had, my, you   (2, 1, 3)

   (d) of, sit, top   (3, 1, 2)

3. **Answers will vary.**

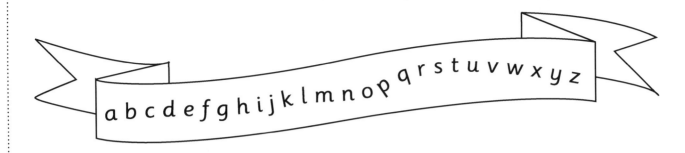

1. Look at the first letter of each word. Circle the word that comes first alphabetically.

(a) | am | big | car | day

(b) | go | it | up | and

(c) | did | bed | see | the

(d) | was | we | on | wet

(e) | if | big | I | is

2. For each line, look at the first letter of each word. Write 1, 2, 3 to show the order.

(a) can ☐   has ☐   to ☐

(b) end ☐   yes ☐   me ☐

(c) my ☐   had ☐   you ☐

(d) top ☐   of ☐   sit ☐

3. (a) Write your first name.

_____

(b) Put a circle around the letter that comes first in the alphabet.

Answers

1. (a) and: hand, band, land, sand

    (b) car: star, jar, far, tar

    (c) end: bend, lend, send, mend

    (d) me: see, be, he, she, we

    (e) sit: lit, fit, bit, hit, pit

    (f) day: say, may, lay, ray, bay

    (g) top: hop, flop, mop, pop

    (h) can: fan, ran, man, van

    (i) wet: set, met, get, jet, let

    (j) look: book, took, cook, hook

2. Possible answers include:

    (a) bed: red, led, fed, wed

    (b) big: dig, fig, jig, pig, rig, wig

    (c) up: cup, pup

    (d) I: by, cry, my, tie, pie

1. Circle the words that rhyme.

(a) | and | hand   band   land   yes   sand

(b) | car | star   can   jar   far   tar

(c) | end | bend   lend   and   send   mend

(d) | me | see   be   by   he   she   we

(e) | sit | sat   lit   fit   bit   hit   pit

(f) | day | say   may   lay   ray   dad   bay

(g) | top | hop   tip   flop   mop   pop   tap

(h) | can | fan   run   ran   man   pin   van

(i) | wet | set   met   meet   get   jet   let

(j) | look | like   book   took   cook   hook

2. Write a word that rhymes with each.

(a) bed _____

(b) big _____

(c) up _____

(d) I _____

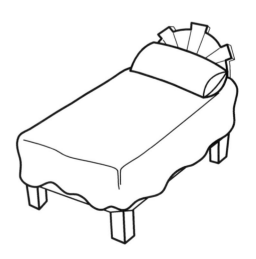

TEACHER INFORMATION

Antonyms are words that are opposite in meaning. Antonyms can add a contrast in description or feeling. Many words take a prefix to create an antonym; e.g. happy – unhappy

Answers

1. (a) small   big

   (b) night   day

   (c) start   end

   (d) stop   go

   (e) off   on

   (f) stand   sit

   (g) bottom   top

   (h) down   up

   (i) dry   wet

   (j) no   yes

2. Teacher check

3. Teacher check

PUPIL NAME

1. Write the word that is opposite.

(a) small _____

(b) night _____

(c) start _____

(d) stop _____

(e) off _____

(f) stand _____

(g) bottom _____

(h) down _____

(i) dry _____

(j) no _____

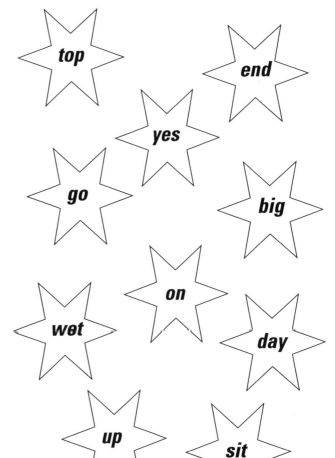

2. Draw a picture of two opposite words.

3. Draw a big dog and a small cat.

TEACHER INFORMATION

Homophones are words that sound the same but have different meanings; e.g. cereal – serial, know – no, feat – feet, stare – stair

Homographs are words that are spelt the same, have different meanings and may or may not sound the same.

Examples:

- bow (rhymes with cow)—a verb meaning to bend the body as a sign of respect
- bow (rhymes with low)—a noun meaning a looped knot

- fair—a noun meaning a group of sideshows
- fair—an adjective meaning not cloudy.

Answers

1. (a) be   (b) bee

2. (a) see   (b) sea

3. (a) to   (b) two

4. (a) for   (b) four

5. (a) red   (b) read

6. (a) one   (b) won

Some words sound the same. Choose one sentence and draw a picture.

PUPIL NAME

1. Write *be* **or** *bee.*

(a) I can _____ the best.

(b) A _____ can buzz.

2. Write *sea* **or** *see.*

(a) I can _____ my dog.

(b) I can swim in the _____.

3. Write *to* **or** *two.*

(a) He is going _____ the shop.

(b) She has _____ legs.

4. Write *for* **or** *four.*

(a) I can get it _____ you.

(b) My dog has _____ legs.

5. Write *red* **or** *read.*

(a) I can draw a _____ ball.

(b) She _____ the book to me.

6. Write *one* **or** *won.*

(a) I have _____ apple.

(b) I _____ the race.

TEACHER INFORMATION

A *capital letter* is used:

- to start a sentence; e.g. She is here today.
- for the pronoun I, including I'm, I've, I'll and I'd
- as the first letter of a proper noun; e.g. Ireland, Thomas, Pacific Ocean
- to start direct speech; e.g. I said, 'She is here today'.
- for the initial letter and proper nouns in titles of books, films etc.; e.g. *Black Beauty, Finding Nemo.*

Prim-Ed Publishing® employs minimal capitalisation for titles of books and other publications, as recommended by the *Style manual for authors, editors and printers,* sixth edition, 2002.

Answers

1. (a) I am on the bed.

   (b) The car is red.

   (c) Look at the dog.

   (d) My cat is black.

   (e) I can see my mum.

   (f) It is the end of the day.

   (g) She went to the play.

   (h) My dad is big.

   (i) He can draw a green ball.

   (j) The shop is shut.

   (k) We are going to the park.

   (l) This is for you.

2. Teacher check

3. Teacher check

A sentence starts with a capital letter.

1. Read each sentence. Use a red pencil to show where the capital letter should be.

(a) i am on the bed.

(b) the car is red.

(c) look at the dog.

(d) my cat is black.

(e) i can see my mum.

(f) it is the end of the day.

(g) she went to the play.

(h) my dad is big.

(i) he can draw a green ball.

(j) the shop is shut.

(k) we are going to the park.

(l) this is for you.

2. Draw four pictures. Match one sentence to each picture.

3. Write a sentence about yourself. Use a capital letter.

TEACHER INFORMATION

A *capital letter* is used:

- to start a sentence; e.g. She is here today.
- for the pronoun I, including I'm, I've, I'll and I'd
- as the first letter of a proper noun; e.g. Ireland, Thomas, Pacific Ocean
- to start direct speech; e.g. I said, 'She is here today'.
- for the initial letter and proper nouns in titles of books, films etc.; e.g. *Black Beauty, Finding Nemo*.

Prim-Ed Publishing® employs minimal capitalisation for titles of books and other publications, as recommended by the *Style manual for authors, editors and printers*, sixth edition, 2002.

Answers

1. (a) I sit next to Ben.

    (b) I like to play with Sam.

    (c) My dad's name is Mark.

    (d) My teacher is Miss Smith.

    (e) I live on West Street.

    (f) We live in Canada.

    (g) Today is Monday.

    (h) Her name is Kate.

    (i) Our school is Parkwood Primary.

    (j) My sisters are Molly and Amy.

    (k) Her brother is Jack.

    (l) Alex is six years old.

2. Teacher check

3. Teacher check

> **A name needs a capital letter.**

1. Use a red pencil to show where the capital letters should be.

(a) I sit next to ben.

(b) I like to play with sam.

(c) My dad's name is mark.

(d) My teacher is miss smith.

(e) I live on west street.

(f) We live in canada.

(g) Today is monday.

(h) Her name is kate.

(i) Our school is parkwood primary.

(j) My sisters are molly and amy.

(k) Her brother is jack.

(l) alex is six years old.

2. Draw four pictures. Match a sentence to each picture.

3. Write your name. Use capital letters.

TEACHER INFORMATION

A *full stop* (.) is used:
- to show the end of a statement; e.g. She went to school.
- for abbreviations when the first part of the word is used; e.g. Feb., Capt.

Answers

1. (a) My dog can bark.

   (b) I can see a star.

   (c) She is going to the park.

   (d) He has a big dog.

   (e) I like milk.

   (f) The grass is green.

   (g) Her name is Lisa.

   (h) Today is Friday.

   (i) I live on Falls Road.

   (j) We have a cat and dog.

   (k) She had to go to the shop.

   (l) My hair is brown.

2. Teacher check

3. Teacher check

A sentence ends with a full stop.

1. Read the sentences. Put in the full stops.

(a) **My dog can bark**

(b) **I can see a star**

(c) **She is going to the park**

(d) **He has a big dog**

(e) **I like milk**

(f) **The grass is green**

(g) **Her name is Lisa**

(h) **Today is Friday**

(i) **I live on Falls Road**

(j) **We have a cat and dog**

(k) **She had to go to the shop**

(l) **My hair is brown**

2. Draw four pictures. Match one sentence to each picture.

3. Write a sentence. Use a full stop.

_____

TEACHER INFORMATION

A *question mark* (?) is used:

- at the end of a sentence that asks a question; e.g. How are you?
- in direct and reported speech where a question is asked; e.g. 'How are you?' she asked.

Answers

1. (a) Is the sky blue?

   (b) Can you see the sky?

   (c) Is today Monday?

   (d) Did you go to the shop?

   (e) Do you like to draw?

   (f) Do you have a pink ball?

   (g) Is your name Oliver?

   (h) Is the grass green?

   (i) Can you ride a bike?

   (j) Is the cat fat?

   (k) Do you have ten toes?

   (l) Is she your Mum?

2. Answers will vary.

3. Teacher check

A question mark (?) is used when a question is asked.

1. Read the sentences. Put in the question marks.

(a) Is the sky blue

(b) Can you see the sky

(c) Is today Monday

(d) Did you go to the shop

(e) Do you like to draw

(f) Do you have a pink ball

(g) Is your name Oliver

(h) Is the grass green

(i) Can you ride a bike

(j) Is the cat fat

(k) Do you have ten toes

(l) Is she your mum

2. Write an answer to the questions.

(a) How old are you?

_____

(b) What number is next?

5, 6, 7, 8, _____

(c) Do you have a sister?

_____

(d) What colour do you like?

_____

(e) What day is it?

_____

(f) What food do you like?

_____

3. Write a question. Use a question mark.

_____

Answers

1. (a) My name is James.

   (b) On Sunday I will go to the park.

   (c) Jess sits next to Dan.

   (d) I like the bike Max has.

   (e) We live at 9 Lake Street.

   (f) Miss Yan read a book.

2. (a) I like to play with my dog.

   (b) Can you sit on a bed?

   (c) Did you see the grey cat?

   (d) My mum has a red car.

   (e) I have two hands.

   (f) Can you see the big ball?

3. (a) Can you ask Jack to play?

   (b) My brother, Aden, is ten.

   (c) The dog's name is Rocky.

   (d) Did you talk to Molly?

PUPIL NAME

1. Use a red pencil to show where the capital letters should be.

(a) my name is james.

(b) on sunday i will go to the park.

(c) jess sits next to dan.

(d) i like the bike max has.

(e) we live at 9 lake street.

(f) miss yan read a book.

2. Use a full stop or a question mark.

(a) I like to play with my dog

(b) Can you sit on a bed

(c) Did you see the grey cat

(d) My mum has a red car

(e) I have two hands

(f) Can you see the big ball

3. Use a red pencil to correct the sentences. You will need to add capital letters, full stops and question marks.

(a) can you ask jack to play

(b) my brother, aden, is ten

(c) the dog's name is rocky

(d) did you talk to molly

TEACHER INFORMATION

Nouns are naming words. They name people, places, things and ideas.

Common nouns are words naming general rather than particular things; e.g. apple, river, table, colour.

Proper nouns name specific people and things and use a capital letter; e.g. England, Luke.

Collective nouns name a group of people, animals or things; e.g. class, herd.

Abstract nouns name an idea, concept or quality; e.g. love, danger, youth, pain.

Nouns are often identified by the placement of *a*, *an*, *the* or *some* in front of the word.

Answers

1. (a) bed   (b) cat   (c) dog

    (d) oranges   (e) pencil   (f) cake

    (g) Sam   (h) baby   (i) books

    (j) tree   (k) chair   (l) bird

2. Teacher check

1. Put a circle around the words that name a person, place or thing.

(a) This is a bed.

(b) The cat is black.

(c) The dog is big.

(d) I like oranges.

(e) My pencil is blue.

(f) This is a cake.

(g) Sam is six.

(h) The baby sleeps.

(i) I like books.

(j) I can draw a tree.

(k) The chair is red.

(l) I can see a bird.

2. (a) Draw two animals.   (b) Draw two things you play with.

TEACHER INFORMATION

A *verb* is a word or group of words that names an action or state of being. Verbs are often called 'doing words'; e.g. read, walks, speak, has broken, ate, will type.

Verbs can indicate tense, voice, mood, number and person.

Answers

1. (a) sit   (b) sleep   (c) see

    (d) draw   (e) drink   (f) eat

    (g) run   (h) read   (i) swim

    (j) watch   (k) walk   (l) throw

2. Teacher check

PUPIL NAME

1. Circle the doing word.

(a) I sit at my desk.

(b) I sleep in my bed.

(c) I see a tree.

(d) I can draw.

(e) I drink milk.

(f) I eat apples.

(g) I can run fast.

(h) I can read.

(i) I like to swim.

(j) I watch television.

(k) I walk to school.

(l) I can throw a ball.

2. (a) Draw one thing you do in the day. Write the doing word.

(b) Draw one thing you do at night. Write the doing word.

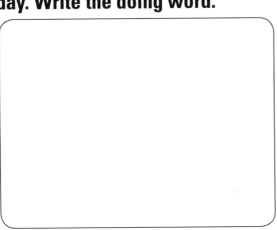

I _____.

I _____.

TEACHER INFORMATION

An *adjective* is a word that describes or gives more information about a noun or pronoun; e.g. pretty, thin, tall, delicious. It qualifies the word it describes by making it more specific; e.g. the red dress—the adjective *red* specifies the colour of the noun *dress*. Adjectives can tell about the colour, size, number, classification or quality of a noun or pronoun. They can come before or after the noun and usually after the pronoun; e.g. the beautiful bird, The bird is beautiful. It is beautiful.

There are three forms of adjectives: absolute (e.g. small), comparative (e.g. smaller), superlative (e.g. smallest).

Answers

1. tree: green, shady, big, tall

2. ball: round, soft, bouncy

3. student: smart, kind, pretty, small

4. apple: tasty, red, crisp, juicy

5. aeroplane: big, loud, heavy, fast

6. Teacher check

Colour the words that can tell about the picture.

1.

green
tall
ten
white
shady
big

2.

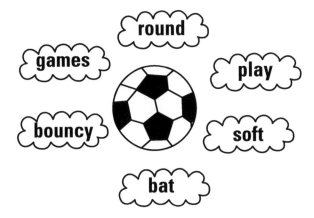

round
games
play
bouncy
soft
bat

3.

me
small
smart
pretty
kind
you

4.

red
tasty
crisp
like
banana
juicy

5.

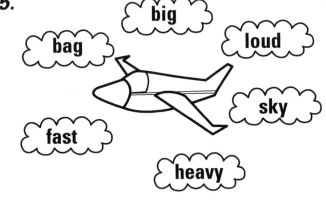

big
bag
loud
sky
fast
heavy

6. **Draw your favourite animal. Write words to describe it.**

PUPIL NAME

TEACHER INFORMATION

A *sentence* is a group of words that makes sense on its own. It must have a finite verb (a verb with a subject), a capital letter at the start, and end in a full stop, question mark or exclamation mark.

Answers

1. (a) I can see the door.

   (b) My mum has a red car.

   (c) I saw a big dog.

   (d) She has two books.

   (e) My dad is kind.

   (f) Can you ride a bike?

   (g) I like my black dog.

   (h) Can we go to the park?

   (i) He has one nose and two feet.

   (j) I will buy a ball at the shop.

1. Write the sentence so it makes sense.

(a) I can see door. the

_____

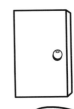

(b) My mum has red car. a

_____

(c) I saw dog. a big

_____

(d) She two books. has

_____

(e) My kind. dad is

_____

(f) Can ride you a bike?

_____

(g) like I my black dog.

_____

(h) we go to Can the park?

_____

(i) He has one feet. and two nose

_____

(j) shop. the at ball a buy will I

_____

TEACHER INFORMATION

A *sentence* is a group of words that makes sense on its own. It must have a finite verb (a verb with a subject), a capital letter at the start, and end in a full stop, question mark or exclamation mark.

Answers

1. Sentences will vary.

1. Finish each sentence so it makes sense.

(a) I like to _____ .

(b) It is fun when _____ .

(c) Today I will _____ .

(d) My teacher is _____ .

(e) I do not like _____ .

(f) At night, I _____ before I
    go to bed.

(g) Jack and Ben _____ .

(h) I am good at _____ .

(i) I eat _____ for breakfast.

(j) On Sunday, I _____ .

(k) I am good at _____ .

(l) I like to _____ after
    school.

TEACHER INFORMATION

A *conjunction* is a word (or words) that connects words, phrases, clauses and sentences; e.g. and, but, because, so, that.

- Conjunctions used to join sentences of equal importance are called coordinating conjunctions; e.g. I like apples and oranges. They include and, but, for, yet, or, as well as, both, so, therefore and nor.

- Conjunctions used to join clauses are called subordinating conjunctions; e.g. She was happy because I arrived. They include because, before, if, while, until, like, though, although, unless, as, since, where, whenever, wherever.

Answers

1. (a) I can run and jump.

   (b) I can talk and walk.

   (c) He can read and write.

   (d) The car is red and fast.

2. (a) I can see the moon but not the sun.

   (b) I like apples but not oranges.

   (c) I can write a sentence but not a book.

   (d) I have two sisters but no brothers.

3. (a) I am tired and I need a sleep.

   (b) I feel sad but I am not crying.

4. Teacher check

1. Use *and* **to join the sentences.**

(a) I can run. I can jump.　　　　　I can run _____ jump.

(b) I can talk. I can walk.　　　　　I can talk _____ walk.

(c) He can read. He can write.　　　He can read _____ write.

(d) The car is red. The car is fast.　The car is red _____ fast.

2. Use *but* **to join the sentences.**

(a) I can see the moon. I can't see the sun.

I can see the moon _____ not the sun.

(b) I like apples. I don't like oranges.

I like apples _____ not oranges.

(c) I can write a sentence. I can't write a book.

I can write a sentence _____ not a book.

(d) I have two sisters. I don't have a brother.

I have two sisters _____ no brothers.

3. Use *and* **or** *but* **to join the sentences.**

(a) I am tired. I need a sleep.

I am tired _____ I need a sleep.

(b) I feel sad. I am not crying.

I feel sad _____ I am not crying.

4. On the back of this sheet, draw a food you like and a food you don't like.

TEACHER INFORMATION

A *sentence* is a group of words that makes sense on its own. It must have a finite verb (a verb with a subject), a capital letter at the start, and end in a full stop, question mark or exclamation mark.

Answers

1. Sentences will vary.

1. Write a sentence. Check if it makes sense. Use a capital letter and full stop.

(a) What did you have for dinner last night?

I had _____ for dinner.

(b) What are you wearing?

I am _____

(c) What animals do you like?

I _____

(d) How many fingers and toes do you have?

_____

(e) What do you like to do on Sunday?

_____

(f) What is your favourite toy?

_____

(g) What sport do you like?

_____

(h) What is your teacher's name?

My _____

PUPIL NAME